The Tongue-in-Cheek Guide to Pittsburgh

Published by

 **W9-DEF-370**

ABELexpress
230 East Main Street
Carnegie, Pennsylvania 15106

PRINTING HISTORY
First printing . . . . April 1992

ATTENTION SCHOOLS & CORPORATIONS

This book, and other products supplied by the Publisher (see inside back cover) are available at quantity discounts with bulk purchases for educational use, business or sales promotion or for fund raising. Special books or book excerpts can also be created to fit specific needs. For details contact the Publisher at the address above.

ISBN 0-944214-01-0
PRINTED IN THE UNITED STATES OF AMERICA

ACKNOWLEDGMENTS

Most books are the work of more than one person. But this book is the work of hundreds of thousands - the people of Pittsburgh without whose funny, but wonderful, special language, much of this book could not have been written. Pittsburghers everywhere: please accept our thanks and appreciation.

In the preparation of any publication, there are always a few people whose help made a difference. So we would like to give our special thanks to:

Adam Pitcock, our graphic artist, who suffered through numerous manuscript revisions and who designed the cover.

Patty Morrison who helped keep everything organized while we waded through the zillions of books, papers and reference materials that are the precursor to any "literary" work.

James V. Battisti, of Pittsburgh, who provided many funny and insightful contributions which appear in this volume.

Our kids, Jeremy, Joshua, Jessica and Joanna, whose comments and questions were the source of several entries in the Glossary and who taught us one very important thing: anyone who gives all their children names starting with the same letter of the alphabet must be totally insane.

To anyone we missed: our apologies and our thanks for helping us in one of the most "fun" projects we have ever been involved with.

HOW TO BECOME A
WORLD FAMOUS AUTHOR
BY HELPING US WRITE VOLUME II

Did you know that there are Pittsburghers in every state . . . and in most foreign countries? Those Pittsburghers - hundreds of thousands of them - all over the world, will be reading *your work* if it is selected for Volume II of *The Tongue-in-Cheek Guide to Pittsburgh*. Here is information on submitting your work.

1. Read each page of Volume I carefully. Laugh . . . or groan . . . or make use of the porcelain facility . . . where appropriate.

2. Compose your own work. It can be additions or changes to what we've printed, or (even better) completely new work of any kind that relates to Pittsburgh and that at least 51% of your friends and family think is funny . . . or at least mildly amusing. Here are a few ideas.

   - Things you might read on the Parkway West overhead message board.
   - What makes Pittsburgh "Someplace Special".
   - "I have some good news and some bad news . . . ."
   - More Pittsburgh phobias.
   - Pittsburgh meanings for some commonly used phrases, sayings, quotations, signs, labels, book and movie titles and. . . .
   - More multiple choice test questions.
   - Funny best and worst of Pittsburgh.
   - Pittsburgh stuff that is too short or too long, too old or too new, too big or too small. . . .
   - More Pittsburgh "Funny Fill-Ins."
   - And, short stories, puzzles, more Glossary definitions, cartoons and . . . .

Offices and businesses are an integral part of Pittsburgh. So those "office humor" sheets that get mailed and FAXed from office to office are worth sending in to us too. Some may be suitable for printing as is, others may need some editing. But if it's funny we'll consider it.

3. a. Submit copies to us for review at the address on page 1. There is no deadline for submissions. However, the sooner you submit your work, the better, since we will publish Volume II as soon as we have accepted enough submissions. Our goal is to have Volume II "on the newstands" for Christmas/Chanukah 1992. If you miss Volume II there will probably be a Volume III and a Volume IV and . . . .

    b. Submit as often as you wish (no boxtops needed with submissions) - one time or ten times, or . . . . *Include your name, address, and day and evening telephone numbers on every submission.*

    c. Anyone can send us their work, including professional writers. What gets published is what's best, no matter what the "credentials" of the author. Even a six year old can make a most amusing - and publishable - observation.

4. Libelous, scatalogical or otherwise unprintable submissions will be thoroughly enjoyed by the staff but cannot be considered for inclusion.

5. Authors of selected submissions will have their names, hometown and other pertinent information listed. For example: "John Smith of Point Breeze," or "Mike Bradley, formerly of Lawrenceville, now living in Palm Springs" or anything else short and reasonable. Authors will *also* receive 2 *gratis* copies of the volume in which their work *first* appears. And finally, selected authors will *also* have the right to purchase additional copies at a specially discounted price.

6. All submissions become the property of the Publisher and cannot be returned or acknowledged and are subject to editing by the Publisher and so on, and so forth, and all that jazz you usually read in the fine print of those silly "complete the jingle" contests.

14 EXCUSES FOR LIVING IN PITTSBURGH

- [ ] My wombat collects Klondike wrappers.
- [ ] Waiting in Parkway traffic gives me plenty of time to do the Sunday New York Times crossword puzzle.
- [ ] It's the only place I can buy Jumbo at Absolute Minimum Pricing.
- [ ] It has two zoos - one in Highland Park and one in the City County Building.
- [ ] I'm a bird fancier and Pittsburgh's a great place to putzie with my sputzies.
- [ ] Living in a city with locations like Youghiogheny and Monongahela makes it easy to practice for the National Spelling Bee.
- [ ] This is my favorite neighborhood . . . won't you be my neighbor.
- [ ] Ah, Pittsburgh! It's great for me. Was it good for you too?
- [ ] I'm waiting to get another boot . . . so I can have a pair.
- [ ] Pizza-burg. That'sa my favorite food.
- [ ] It's the only town ALWAYS under construction.
- [ ] Rand McNally was right!
- [ ] In Pittsburgh, you can have it all.
- [ ] Pittsburgh? Did you say *PITTSBURGH*! Omigod, I thought this was Yuba City, California.
- [ ] So, who needs an excuse!

IMPORTANT PITTSBURGH TELEPHONE NUMBERS

In these days of fast food and short memories, consumers need help in remembering important telephone numbers. Clever businesses and government agencies are aware of this and select telephone numbers which spell out simple, easy to remember words or phrases. Here are some suggested telephone numbers which could be used to help Pittsburghers remember what to dial when they need service.

State Police Parkway Traffic Control	412-DRIV-SLO
Department of Parks and Recreation	412-MANY-PARKS
City Controllers Office	412-GET-SUED
Gateway Clipper Reservation Office	412-LOTSA-BOATS
Pittsburgh Police River Patrol	412-NO-BOATS
PPG Place Maintenance Office	412-LOTSA GLAS
Pittsburgh Aviary	412-LOTSA-BIRDS
Pan Am Airlines	412-NO-BIRDS
Mayor's Office	412-BOSS-LADY
Overdue Parking Ticket Patrol	412-DAS-BOOT
WPXI News Anchor Desk	412-WHOS-NEW
Pittsburgh Press	412-ADS-R-US
Pittsburgh Pirates Baseball Team	412-PLAY-BALL
Pittsburgh Steelers Football Team	412-NEW-COACH
Pittsburgh Spirit Soccer Team	412-SAY-WHAT
Pittsburgh Penguins Hockey Team	412-WINTR-BOYS

(The number you have dialed, 412-WINTR-BOYS, has been changed. The new number is 412-WINTR-MEN. Please make a note of it.)

Pittsburgh Brewing Company	412-BIG-SUDS
The Pound	412-BAD-DAHG
The Other Pound	412-LOSE-UR-CAR
The Pitt Tunnel Info Line	412-TUBE-TALK
Wind Symphony	412-WATR-MUSIC

NICKNAMES AND MOTTOS

When we read these *actual* nicknames or mottos . . .

. . . it makes us think of these *possible* nicknames or mottos.

Rome's Nickname:
The Eternal City

The Parkway's Motto:
The Eternal Nightmare

Paris' Nickname:
The City of Lights

Pittsburgh: *The City of Lighting Bills from the Electric Utility with the Highest Rates in the Country.*

Alabama's Motto:
God Enriches

City Controller's Office Motto:
The Controller's Office enriches

California's Motto:
Eureka (I have found it)

Pennsylvania Tax Dep't's Motto:
Good, now we'll take it away

Georgia's Motto:
Wisdom, Justice and Moderation

Pennsylvania's Motto:
Sorry, but nothing comes to mind

Minnesota's Nickname:
Land of Ten Thousand Lakes

Pittsburgh's Nickname:
Land of Ten Thousand Potholes

Texas' Motto:
The Eyes of Texas are Upon You

Pennsylvania's Motto:
Our Eyes and Taxes are Upon You

Boy Scouts' Motto:
Be Prepared

Pennsylvania's Motto:
State of Disrepair

Old U.S. Motto:
Liberty Forever

Pittsburgh's Motto:
~~Democracy~~ Democrats Forever

Denny's Restaurants' Motto:
We Never Close

PennDOT Parkway Motto:
We Never Close . . . Except When It Rains or Snows or Gets Damp or Windy

PITTSBURGH DOUBLESPEAK

We all use euphemisms - words that sound better or less offensive than the words they replace. *Doublespeak* is a non-eumphemistic word for the euphemisms of government and business. Here are some apocryphal examples of *Doublespeak* which Pittsburghers might actually welcome as an interesting alternative to the phrases they are currently exposed to.

This often repeated situation might not sound so bad if it were replaced with . . .	. . . this phrase
Parkway pileup.	Multivehicular exterior interaction.
Riot after rock concert at Point State Park.	Non-harmonious civic assemblage.
A lie, told by a major Pittsburgh corporation, after it has been uncovered by the media.	Terminological inexactitude.
Permanent layoffs.	Career alternative enhancement programs.
Flooding of the Mon Parking Wharf.	Aqueous overload at the mortar-air interface.
Drive-by shooting in Pittsburgh.	Unanticipated antagonist extirpation initiative.
Lousy Holiday Season sales in Pittsburgh area retail stores.	4th quarter procurement languor.
Agents acting for Pittsburgh sports personalities who negotiate megabuck contracts for their clients.	Personal performance remuneration specialists.

PITTSBURGH PHOBIAS

This *actual* phobia is the basis for ...

... this *unique* phobia in residents of Pittsburgh

spermatophobia: fear of germs

monongospermophobia: fear of being swallowed by a sperm whale while swimming in the Monongahela River

gynephobia: fear of women

mayorogynephobia: fear of women mayors

phasmophobia: fear of ghosts

pennsyphasmophobia: fear of being found out as a ghost employee on the payroll in Pennsylvania

taurophobia: fear of bulls
coprophobia: fear of feces

taurocoprophobia: fear of local politicians

parasitophobia: fear of parasites

federoparasitophobia: fear of national politicians

rhabdophobia: fear of magic

gubernorabdophobia: governor's fear that the citizens will realize he is trying to use magic instead of common sense to balance the budget

kenophobia: fear of voids
politicophobia: fear of politics

craniopoliticokenophobia: fear that the public will realize how empty headed most politicians are

ornithophobia: fear of birds

electomayorornithophobia: mayor's fear that her fear of birds will lead to the voters' fear of electing her again

thaasophobia: fear of being idle

pennsythaasophobia: state employees' fear that they will run out of work to do so that they will be collecting pay for doing absolutely nothing (right!)

gephyrophobia: fear of crossing a bridge

trollogephyrophobia: fear of being eaten by a troll when you cross a typical, about-to-collapse, Pittsburgh bridge

ancraophobia: fear of wind
chionophobia: fear of snow
cheimatophobia: fear of cold
thermophobia: fear of heat
homichlorophobia: fear of fog

ancraochionocheimatothermohomichloro-Joesophobia: Joes's fear that it won't be hot, cold, windy, snowy or foggy, even though he said it would

apeirophobia: fear of infinity

apeirofoliophobia: fear that this page will go on forever

9

PITTSBURGH TRAFFIC SIGNS & SIGNALS

Some fun stuff from James V. Battisti of Pittsburgh, our most prolific contributor. What very special traffic signs can *you* come up with for Volume II?

CHANGE YOUR MIND ZONE

MAJOR INTERSECTIONS

TRAFFIC JAM AHEAD TURN AROUND

NO DANCING ZONE

CHEERLEADER XING
(Found Near Colleges)

I MADE IT!

HAND SIGNALS

RIGHT HERE! BUDDY!

I DON'T KNOW WHICH WAY TO GO!!

FUNNY FILL-INS

Here's a game that can be played by two or more people. It's fun and can be played again and again with totally different results every time.

Below is a story with blank spaces where words have been left out. The *Reader* does not tell the other *Players* anything about the story - not even its title. The *Reader* simply asks the other *Players* to supply the missing words. The *Reader* asks each *Player,* in turn, to call out a word - a noun, adjective or other part of speech - appropriate for that blank space. When all the spaces are filled the *Reader* reads the completed story aloud. The other *Players* will hear that they have written a story that may be silly, or crazy, or shocking, or even dumb . . . but usually always funny.

Here is a quick review of some of the types of words - parts of speech - that are used in this *Funny Fill-In.*

> **Noun:** A person, place, thing or relationship. Toilet, banana, doorstep, address, brother, establishment, janitor and aardvark are nouns.

> **Adjective:** Qualifies a noun or makes it more exact. Yellow, greasy, radical, fat, listless, pedantic, sensitive, and dumb are adjectives.

> **Verb:** Indicates action, state or being; but action verbs are the best to use in *Funny Fill-Ins.* A second person singular verb is the form after *you,* as in *you stink.* A third person singular verb is the form after, *he, she,* or *it,* as in *it stinks.*

> **Gerund:** The form of a verb ending in-*ing.* Jumping, screaming, sucking, exposing and living are gerunds.

The other parts of speech are obvious; so you are now ready to start "filling in." Have fun. (Hint: photocopy the page *before* "filling in" so you can use it again and again with different groups of *Players.*

A DAY AT KENNYWOOD PARK

Kennywood Park is a fun place to visit on a/an _____

adjective

summer day. When you arrive at the gate, you whip out your

_____ and give the ticket taker a/an _____ to

noun   noun

pay for your admission. The most famous ride at Kennywood

Park is the _____ _____ and that's where you go

gerund   noun

first. Unfortunately, the ride is really fast and it makes you

_____. After you recover, you get really hungry so

verb - 2nd person singular

you stop at the _____ for a bite to eat. You order a bowl

noun

of _____, an ear of buttered _____, and a

liquid   noun

delicious _____ _____, with mustard and relish.

adjective - size   noun

After eating it is time for more rides. First you put on your

_____ and ride through the Raging Rapids. With all that

noun

_____ splashing around, you get very wet. So after the

liquid

ride you sit in the sun to dry off your _____ and your

body part

_____. Your next stop is the Log Jammer which is a very

body parts

_____ ride. Your log moves slowly at first, then it gets

adjective

to the top and _____ down to the bottom.
verb - 3rd person singular

_____, you exclaim, as you come to a sudden stop.
exclamation

Now it's off to the Bumper Cars in which you drive around until

you run into _____ driven by _____. Next, it's
plural noun   plural noun

the Merry-Go-Round, where you sit on a big _____ that
noun

moves up and down. All that exertion makes you thirsty so you

stop and grab a quick drink of _____ and move on to the
liquid

roller coaster. You jump into the first available car and sit down

in the _____. _____ jumps in next to you and
noun   person

the ride begins. _____, you yell, as the roller coaster
exclamation

rounds the first bend and your _____ flies off. The ride
noun

is thrilling, as you go _____ over the track, but it finally
gerund

comes to an end and you get out. Its about time to leave so you

make your last stop at the concession stand to grab a quick bite of

_____ _____. Then you get into your
animal   body parts

_____ and drive home after a wonderful day at
noun

Kennywood Park.

INTERESTING STUFF ABOUT PENNSYLVANIA

You know how it happens. You step into a room and there are 4 or 5 people in a corner, all chuckling. You walk over to see what's so funny and discover that they are passing around a sheet of paper with some words and crude drawings. Usually the paper is a copy of a copy of a copy of a copy . . . making it verrrrrry hard to read. But you get it, and you read it, and you chuckle too.

That's exactly how the drawings below came into our possession. We don't know the author so we have no one to credit and no one to thank. We've "cleaned it up" to make it easier to read and pass it on to you for your amusement.

WELCOME TO PENNSYLVANIA

The State Where Every Highway Eventually Narrows To A Single Lane Or Is . . .

STATE ANIMAL
The Barrier Horse

STATE HISTORICAL LANDMARK

STATE MINERAL

STATE FLAG

STATE STATUE

STATE MOTTO

STATE TREE

STATE JOKE

Pittsburghese is what we call it. It's that special language-within-a-language that is unique to Pittsburgh. Oh sure, people in Boston and Brooklyn and Tupelo talk "funny" too. But *Pittsburghese* is different. *Pittsburghese* is words that don't seem to exist anywhere else, like *grinny* and *sputzie* and *redd up* and *yunz*. *Pittsburghese* is words we *think* we've heard elsewhere - like *dahntahn* and *Ahiya* and *hosale* - but we're just not really sure. And of course, *Pittsburghese* is those special Pittsburgh-only words like *chippedchopped ham*, *Smiffilled*, *Robison* and *Scroll Hill*.

Some people might call it a dialect. Others might call it regional English. But to all of us, it's just plain *Pittsburghese*. Here, for your edification and amusement is a glossary of *Pittsburghese* people, places and things. As with any listings, there will be omissions. So we leave it to you, our readers, to help us compile a *complete* glossary by submitting your words and definitions for publication in Volume II.

Absolute Minimum Pricing

1. A method of saving money on the purchase of your Thanksgiving turkey, which could be described as *getting the bird at the Big Bird without having a bird.* See also: ***Jynt Iggle***.

Ahiya

1. A special greeting used by Pittsburghers when they unexpectedly meet one of our neighbors from the west.

Ahl

1. A small, pointed tool.

2. A narrow passageway or corridor.

3. A large winged, forest dweller with big round eyes, that sees quite well in the dark, has a dietary preference for mice, and

upon sighting a human, invariably inquires as to *"who, who"* they are.

AHT

1. You've probably heard of the food preservative *BHT*; well ***AHT*** was what they tried first, that didn't work. We hear they're working now on *CHT* and *DHT*, not to be confused with *DDT, DOT* or *DEET*.

2. A Pittsburgher's way of saying *out*, as in *"Don't **wait dinner** for me honey, I'm going **aht** for a walk."*

Airport Parking

1. An arrangement that must have been suggested by Al Capone or Jesse James wherein anyone at an airport parking meter pays 25¢ for just 7-1/2 minutes of time. The meters are placed in locations far enough from the airport gates, such that your time runs out - and you get a parking citation - just about 3 minutes before you get back to your car.

The price of 25¢ for 7-1/2 minutes of parking time works out to a rental of $17,520 per year for each parking space. The average parking space measures about 9' x 15', so the rental cost in real estate terms, is about $130 per square foot. And you thought it was expensive to rent office space *dahntahn*! At least you get a bathroom when you rent *dahntahn*!

ALCOSAN

1. A rather large mechanical contrivance constructed by Allegheny County to prove their theory that what goes in must come out.

Alls

1. An example of a grammatical construction peculiar to Pittsburgh in which a letter of the alphabet is added to a word for no apparent reason. *Alls* means the same as *all*. For example: "*We may have to go out to dinner tonight; alls I have left in the refrigerator is some stale bread and an*

open jar of strawberry jelly."

All The Further

1. Pittsburghers love lots of things - Iron City Beer, a ride on the Incline, and the view from the Fort Pitt Bridge as you enter Pittsburgh, to name just three. But one of the things that Pittsburghers love the most is the word **all.** Pittsburghers use **all** in many strange ways . . . from simply adding an *s* for no apparent reason (see **alls,** above), to making up an entire phrase revolving around that universal word. *All the further* is an example of a complete phrase designed around the word **all,** as in *"I started driving to Philadelphia but it started to snow and Harrisburg was* **all the further** *I got."* (Note, in addition, the use of the word **got,** a well known favorite of teachers of English throughout the world.)

Anymore

1. A rather confusing construction which doesn't mean *any,* or *more,* or even *anymore.*

Instead it means *nowadays*, or *currently*, or *these days*. It almost always occurs as the first word of a sentence, as in this example: **"Anymore**, *the traffic on Liberty Avenue moves so slowly, it's quicker to walk.*"

The Arena
See: **Civic Arena**

Arn
See: **Hoist**

Ashfault
1. The streets of Pittsburgh are covered with a black tar-like material, in which potholes tend to appear during the winter months, due to the combined effects of the heavy snows and of the salt used to melt that snow. The head of the Street Maintenance Department for the City of Pittsburgh, John Ash, does his best to get the potholes repaired before motorists' cars hit them, causing damage to the cars and their tires.

Unfortunately, the potholes frequently form faster than the Street Maintenance crew can repair them. Thus, when a car sustains damage from a pothole and the insurance adjustor asks what caused the problem, the usual answer is, *"It's that damn **Ashfault**."*

This problem should be distinguished from somewhat similiar difficulties which have been found to occur occasionally in southern California, an area far from where Mr. Ash does his work. In southern California car damage is caused by earthquakes rather than by potholes. Thus, when insurance adjustors examine damaged vehicles and ask whose fault it is, the response is usually, *"San Andreas fault."*

Aviary

1. A Pittsburgh educational center and attraction unique in this country in that it is the only such indoor facility not part of a zoological park. The Aviary contains birds of every description, including many tropical species, from every continent except Antarctica.

The Aviary was in the news in 1991 and 1992 because of the dispute between the bird *lovers* in the City limits who wanted to keep the Aviary running, and the bird *brains* in the City government who wanted to shut it down.

It has been suggested that perhaps Mayor Sophie Masloff, who was apparently behind the City's campaign to close the Aviary, might be persuaded to visit the Aviary during feeding time to see all the birds, especially the giant condor that inhabits one of the outdoor cages. However, that idea was abandoned when it was concluded that the meat would be tough and stringy and would probably give the condor indigestion.

Use this space for making smart-aleck comments about our work . . . or for composing your own submissions for Volume II.

Barges

1. Large flat bottomed craft used for transporting coal and other commodities on the navigable rivers, having a seemingly magnetic attraction for Pittsburgh bridges, around which they wrap themselves with some frequency.

Bath

1. The shortage of pencils in the early days of Pittsburgh history caused many Pittsburghers to leave "unnecessary" letters out of words so that their pencils would last longer. Thus, the *e* was left out of ***bathe*** and over time, Pittsburghers changed the pronounciation from a long *a* sound (***bathe***) to a short *a* sound (***bath***). Thus Pittsburghers now say *"I'm going to **bath** the baby."*

Beer

1. A frothy, yellow, liquid substance rented by men, for a short period of time. See also: *Arn* and *Iron*

Bee-You´-Tee-Full

1. Pittsburghers frequently slur their words, but this one comes through loud and clear - all 4 syllables of this, usually, 3 syllable word. Only in Pittsburgh can they pronounce it *bee-you´-tee-full*. And if you think this sounds strange, read on a few pages and see what Pittsburghers do to the pronunciation of the name of a little yellow weed they find in their yards in the Springtime.

Bloomfilled

1. You've heard of the *Field of Dreams* and the *Killing Fields*. And even *Forbes Field* and *Sally Field*. This is a field of flowers - or blooms. Hence the name Bloomfield (as they call it in Harrisburg) or *Bloomfilled* (as they call it in Pittsburgh). Actually we don't know if there are any flowers in *Bloomfilled*, so just drive down to this

well known Pittsburgh neighborhood and you can find out for yourself.

Bock´man

1. When spelled, **Bachman**, a crispy pretzel of sterling quality, that crunches in your teeth with a deep vibrant tone.

2. When spelled, **Baughman**, a morning news personality, with a sterling voice that glides through your ears with a deep vibrant tone. It is probably not a coincidence that **Baughman** rhymes with **Talkman**. Not to be confused with the also-rhyming, **Walkman**, which is smaller and lighter than a **Baughman**, and which doesn't answer back when spoken to.

Boilermaker

1. A student or graduate of Purdue University.

2. A drink common to the steelworkers who formerly plied their trade in Pittsburgh, consisting of a shot of whiskey poured into

a beer. Currently, some people also consider a beer with a whiskey chaser, to be a **boilermaker**.

Buggy

1. **Full of bugs**, as in *"I left an open box of cereal on the counter for two days and now it's all **buggy**."*

2. **A little crazy**, as in *"It was 92° in the shade and John went out into the field to cut down that big apple tree. He must be **buggy**."*

3. **Something used to carry babies**, as in *"John. Look what I got at the baby shower; a beautiful baby **buggy**."*

4. **One of those metal or plastic 4-wheeled shopping carts available in supermarkets for gathering groceries**, as in *"Norman, for goodness sake! You can't carry all those groceries in your arms! Go get a **buggy** to put them in."*

Carnegie

See: *Kernegie*

Carnegie Institute of Technology (C.I.T)

1. The original name for what is now known as Carnegie Mellon University.

The Carnegie

1. In Pittsburgh, a museum, a library and an institute.

2. In Manhattan, a delicatessen named after a famous Pittsburgher.

3. Also in Manhattan, a big hall which, unlike Pittsburgh halls, does *not* host bingo parties and wedding receptions, but rather, ballets and symphonies. Named after the famous Andrew Carnegie.

Catch Up

1. The kind of ball that ball teams play when they are not winning.

2. What ball team members and others, put on their hot dogs and french fries and (for those with dysfunctional taste buds), on their scrambled eggs.

Cathedral of Learning

1. This enormous building is the centerpiece of the Pitt campus. So named because parents are frequently seen praying in the shadow of the *Cathedral*, that their children will be graduated and move on to a high salary job so that they can help pay back the enormous sums that their parents spent to put them through college in the first place.

2. Due to the fact that many people work late hours in that building, fortified with food from the local Italian restaurants, it has also been known to be called the *Learning Tower of Pizza.*

Cellar

1. A place of safety sought by Pittsburgh residents in the event of tornados.

2. A place of danger avoided by some Pittsburgh sports teams which have nevertheless found themselves locked there in the recent past.

Cherry Tart

1. A breakfast menu item in some Pittsburgh restaurants.

2. A contradiction in terms.

Chippedchopped Ham

1. A Pittsburgh "delicacy" which is made by taking one of those large, rectangular gray colored "hams" (you know, the ones with the labels that say *water added*, and you wonder whether the water came from the Ohio River or maybe New York's East River) and which is chopped and shredded so you can make ***sammiches*** with a big lump in the center.

Chivie

1. A car, specifically one made by the Chevrolet Division of General Motors Corporation.

Circus

1. Something that went well with bread in ancient Rome.

2. Something that the Ringling Brothers and Misters Barnum and Bailey are famous for.

3. Pittsburgh City Council meetings, as described by many local observers. Based on the content of some of the council meetings, as reported by the media, it has been suggested that the Council hang a 4' x 8' sheet of plywood at the front of their meeting room, on which is printed, in very large letters, *"Engage brain before putting mouth in gear."* For the same reasons that led to this suggestion, City Council meetings are frequently referred to as a "zoo." See also: *Zoo*.

City Chicken

1. A unique Pittsburgh dish, said by some to be quite tasty. It consists of alternating chunks of veal and pork impaled on a wooden skewer.

2. A dish similiar to what is described in definition (1), but which is made from lower cost, more accessible, ingredients, for which reason it is sometimes known as *City Pigeon*.

Civic Arena

1. A large, dome shaped arena used for sporting events and noted for having a retractable roof which can be opened to the sky, exposing sports fans to the sun, bugs, ill mannered teen agers and occasional torrential downpours. The roof is not opened often because the cost of doing so is just slightly higher than the National Debt of a certain South American country which does *not* export cocaine. (Yes, there really is one such country.)

Clark Bar

1. An establishment in which Clark Kent and General Mark Clark would have been likely to hang out.

2. A chocolate covered confection which originated in Pittsburgh. The Clark Candy company was recently sold and everyone was concerned that the company would Leaf the City; but that problem was eventually resolved.

Cleveland

1. What most Pittsburghers think of when asked to describe how bad Pittsburgh used to be. Rumor has it that Cleveland, tiring of all the snide comments made about it by Pittsburgh, is developing a tactical nuclear missile which will be aimed at Pittsburgh's most vulnerable location - the place where the movers and shakers of the City congregate (the McDonald's on Stanwix Street).

2. The site of a large Armory . . . or is that an Amory, . . . or . . . . oh, forget it.

The Club

1. Every male over the age of 21 in Pittsburgh has a **club** to go to. **Clubs** are places in which you find inexpensive hard liquor, freely flowing **Arn**, and a lot of old guys reminiscing about the "good old days," when the guy who swept the floor in the **mill** made more money than the presidents of many modern day Pittsburgh Corporations.

Comere

1. A Pittsburgh "quickie". *Come here*, said quickly, is **comere.** See also: **Gahed.**

Commonwealth

1. A word refering to the political makeup of Pennsylvania. Derived from the words **wealth** meaning, *riches*, and **common**, meaning *divided among the populace*. Clearly a misnomer.

Cot Also: *Caht*

1. Anywhere in the U.S.A., a small bed.

2. In Pittsburgh, the past tense of *catch*.

Crew´ - sant

1. A crescent shaped bread product known, by the uninitiated, as a *croissant.*

Crick

1. The use of **crick** for *creek* is not restricted to our neighbors down South, as anyone listening to a Pittsburgher describing **Chartiers Crick** can tell you. Let's just hope nobody twists his head after falling in the water, lest he be forced to tell us *"I got a crick in my neck from falling in the crick."*

Crookit

1. That's what most politicians and all dogs' hind legs are. If you think **crookit** sounds funny, try saying **crookit crick** three times, fast.

Cupbird

1. A container, usually filled with food or water, placed in a bird cage. This object is

also sometimes called a *birdcup* instead of
cupbird.

2. In Pittsburgh, a closet or cabinet for storage,
   as in **kitchen cupbird**, which is where one
   might store dishes or food or . . . .

Use this space for making smart-aleck comments about our work . . . or for composing your own submissions for Volume II.

D

1. Pittsburghers have a lot of strange likes and dislikes. One dislike is the letter **D**, especially when it is in the middle of a word, next to another consonant.

Being non-violent, for the most part, Pittsburghers do not rely on force to eliminate those offensive **D**'s; instead they simply invoke one of the laws of English pronunciation and make the **D**'s silent.

Hence, *couldn't* becomes ***cooun't***, *wouldn't* becomes ***wooun't***, and everyone's all time favorite, *didn't* becomes ***din't***.

Dahntahn

1. Imagine if Petula Clark had been born in

Pittsburgh. And that she recorded a tune called **Dahntahn**, that you would be listening to for 20 years. Horrible thought, isn't it! The nasal sound exemplified by the word ***dahntahn*** can be heard issuing from Pittsburgh natives of all ages - especially older ones whose sinuses have been dissolved by the atmosphere that formerly pervaded the City.

Dan´- dee - lion

1. Something Richard the Lion Hearted would have liked.

2. Something any lion tamer would like.

3. A lioness' mane man.

4. The main ingredient in lyonnaise potatoes.

5. Something Daniel prayed for when he was thrown into the lion's den.

6. They aren't "dandy" if you're the one that

has to weed the garden but we wouldn't be "lyin'" if we said there are loads of those little yellow babies popping up all over Pittsburgh as soon as Spring weather graces the City. To paraphrase a famous author, *"A tree grows in Brooklyn, but **dan-dee-lions** grow in Pittsburgh."*

Deja Vu

1. The feeling experienced by Republicans every Election Day when the results of the mayoral race for the City of Pittsburgh are announced.

Denver Boot

1. A unique memory aid, recently introduced by the Pittsburgh Police, to help Pittsburgh motorists recall how many unpaid parking tickets they have accumulated.

Dill

1. You know, as in *"Let's make a **dill**"* and, *"Boy, have I got a **dill** for you."* Lots of good ***dills*** can be had in ***the Strip***, where the

many food wholesalers open their shops to the public on Sunday. But be careful of those sidewalk vendors; if you don't know what you're buying, your *dill* could get you into a real pickle!

Disaster

1. What happens in other cities, that the Emergency Management Team fervently hopes will not happen in Pittsburgh.

2. What happened when a young lady backed into an airplane propellor at Pittsburgh International Airport.

Djeatyet? Nodju?

1. No, this is not Polish or Ukrainian. It's those Pittsburghers again, spitting out syllables as fast as they can and losing half of them in the process. Complete translation below.

   Djeatyet? = Question: *"Did you eat yet?"*
   Nodju? = Answer: *"No. Did you?"*

Don

1. The opposite of up.

2. Early in the a.m., as in *"the **don's** early light."*

3. At Christmastime, what we do with our gay apparel.

4. Someone who hails from Sicily, and who would be happy to make you an offer you couldn't refuse.

Drug

1. No, it's not something that the President's Commission on Crime in America needs to investigate, it's simply the past tense of *drag*, as in *"I saw our dog running down the street so I grabbed his leash and **drug** him in."*

Use this space for making smart-aleck comments about our work . . . or for composing your own submissions for Volume II.

Face the Musick

1. A unique form of punishment formerly meted out by *The Pittsburgh Press* newspaper to anyone who trampled on the dignity or sensibilities of Pittsburghers.

Fer (not to be confused with "fur.")

1. *Fer* is a more or less acceptable substitute for the word *for* except when quoting Dickens, since, as everyone can see, *"'Tis a fer, fer better thing that I do, than I have ever done,"* sounds a bit ludicrous.

Ferris Wheel

1. A small bunch of iron bearing minerals, arranged horizontally on the ground in the shape of a circle, frequently described by the alternate spelling *Ferrous Wheel.*

2. A large bunch of people bearing containers, arranged vertically in the air, in the shape of a circle, invented by George W. Ferris.

Filum

1. An American Indian word for the photo-sensitive product used in cameras. As for example, what Tonto says to the Lone Ranger when he spies some scantily clad Indian maidens batheing in the **crick.** *"Quick, Kemo Sabe. You givum **filum** to me, so I can getum some skin shots."*

Flaherty

1. A generic term for Pittsburgh polititian.

2. An old Gaelic phrase which translates loosely as *"You can't fool all of the people all of the time."*

Flood Stage

1. An imaginary line which is at least two feet lower than the water level of Pittsburgh's rivers, on several recent occasions.

Gahed

1. Say it quick in Pittsburgh and it's not *go ahead*, but rather **gahed**. See also: **Comere**.

Gedaht!

1. A shortened form of **Gedahtahere**! this exclamation is not something you yell at the dog when he makes a mess on the rug, but rather an exclamation of surprise, synonomous with such equally colorful phrases as *"I didn't know that,"* *"Really?"* (or in Pittsburgh, **Rilly**!), the obsolete *"Gee whiz!"* the archaic *"Pshaw,"* the ever popular, *"No kidding!"* and the not-fit-for-print, *"No s_ _ _!"*

Get a Bath

1. Ever wonder why it is that when

Pttsburghers invite their out-of-town friends and relatives to stay for a few days that their kids are always dirty? It's because you keep telling them to **get a bath** - and they have no idea where to look for one. (Maybe you'll have more luck with *get a life*.) In most other places people **take** baths and showers, in Pittsburgh, people **get** them.

Giardia Lambia

1. An obscure American Indian proverb dating from the days of William Pitt, whose meaning is not totally clear to historians, but possibly referring to a small body of water which no longer exists. Literally translated as: *"You-drink-um water-you-up-Shitz-Creek."*

Going For

1. This phrase is used in conjunction with the time, as in *"You'd better hurry or you'll be late for work. It's **going for** eight o'clock."*

Great Flood of 1936

1. A constant reminder to the businesses in **dahntahn** Pittsburgh and to the Army Corps of Engineers that *"man proposes, but God disposes."*

Greenfilled

1. A tune by Ralph Vaughn Williams made famous after words were put to it. *("Alas, my love, you do me wrong, to cast me off discourteously ....")*

2. A Pittsburgh neighborhood, adjacent to **Scroll Hill**, which is very urban and thus has few fields and very little green, other than the cemetary located within it.

Green Tree Hill

1. A thermometer stuck in Pittsburgh's backside which measures automotive congestion by the degree to which it is covered with traffic.

Grinny

1. A contraction of the words for a thin grandmother, *i.e.*, a granny who is skinny, or a ***grinny***.

2. A person who is prone to grinning.

3. A chipmunk. A *chipmunk*? Yep, Pittsburghers, that's what it is. But we don't know why it is, so the first person with some answers - real or tongue-in-cheek - on the origin of ***grinny*** is assured a place in Volume II.

Gumban

1. A word which, if said slowly, would be heard as ***gum band***, which is a Pittsburgher's term for what Easterners (and most everyone else in the world) call a *rubber band*. The term may have resulted from a shortening of the name of the material from which these were originally made - gum rubber. Thus, while everyone else in the world shortened *gum rubber band* to *rubber band*,

Pittsburghers, with their unique sense of originality, shortened it to **gum band**. This of course, is only a theory.

Gum bands should not be confused with the similiar sounding *gummy bears*. The differences are obvious. **Gum bands** are weirdly shaped, strange tasting, non-edible objects; whereas gummy bears are weirdly shaped, strange tasting, barely-edible objects.

Use this space for making smart-aleck comments about our work . . . or for your own submissions for Volume II.

Hafer, Barbara

1. Bob Casey's worst nightmare.

Haffing

1. Usually used in connection with the word *to*, as in *"I sent my payment in by mail, so I could settle up my account without **haffing** to go there."*

Hans

1. Handsome young Norwegian men with blue eyes and blonde hair are named ***Hans***.

2. Something each Pittsburgher has two of, and on each of them are five fingers.

seeing, and most especially, speaking of any evil he claims to have been perpetrated **by** those Penguins.

Hoagy

1. What Mr. Carmichael ate.

2. What everyone in Pittsburgh calls a submarine **sammich**.

Hoist

1. A device used by iron workers to move large and/or heavy objects from the ground up to a building under construction.

2. A move used by **Arn** drinkers to propel tankards and/or bottles from the counter up to their lips.

(Note how times have changed in Pittsburgh. The elimination of the steelmaking industry has so changed mental processes in Pittsburghers, that **Arn** no longer refers to the giant iron girders with which great ships and buildings were constructed, but now refers only to a beer supplied by a local brewery.)

Visitors to Pittsburgh report a strange custom in which male **Arn** drinkers "adopt" a water dwelling animal such as a salamander or iguana at the Pittsburgh Zoo. Then, after consuming three or more beers, these drinkers are overcome by an irresistable urge to return to the zoo where they ***hoist*** their adopted pets out of the water, a strange ritual known as *draining their lizard.*

Ho´-Sale

1. How Santa Claus gets rid of his excess inventory of *Ho Ho Ho's* after Christmas.

2. A special offering, at discount prices, of ladies of the evening.

3. This is how Pittsburgh retailers like to buy.

How big of a

1. This phrase is sort of like ***those ones***, in that sometimes Pittsburghers just don't know when to stop during a sentence - they include one or two unnecessary words. The response to *"I caught a really big fish on the lake yesterday,"* should be, *"Oh, how big a fish was it?"* But in Pittsburgh, the response is *"**How big of a** fish was it?"*

Use this space for making smart-aleck comments about our work . . . or for your own submissions for Volume II.

I

Ice Balls

1. A non-infectious physiological condition to which male Pittsburghers are especially vulnerable during the winter months.

2. Pittsburghers' name for a confection consisting of a ball of ice chips saturated with a sugary syrup of any of various flavors. Known in some areas as a *snow cone*.

Ignernt

1. Here's a word guaranteed to confuse any new arrival to Pittsburgh. To everyone else the word *ignorant* (whence ***ignernt*** derives) means uninformed or lacking in knowledge. But in Pittsburgh, ***ignernt*** means rude.

Thus, because Pittsburghers are a very polite and friendly lot, if ever they feel a need to say something that they are concerned that you may take offense at, they start the sentence with *"I'm not trying to be ignernt, but . . . ."* For example, in commenting on your choice of apparel for a formal dinner they might say *"I'm not trying to be ignernt but that chartreuse shirt doesn't quite seem to match those fuschia trousers."*

People who are delibertely *ignernt* run the risk of being called *jagoffs*. See: *Jagoff.*

Indian Names
1. The Red Man inhabited Western Pennsylvania long before the White Man even thought about what might lie beyond Manhattan Island. After the settlers began arriving in Western Pennsylvania, and logically enough, settling (isn't that what settlers are supposed to do?), they befriended the natives, introducing them to such benefits of Western Civilization as smallpox and dipththeria, racism and xenophobia.

Pragmatic people that they were, the Indians named their geographic locations after terrain features, giving rise to many long and hard to pronounce words and also to a plethora of bad jokes, some sort of silly (*"... and, this is my son Luke,"*) and some sort of not fit for repetition in polite company (*"... yes, my son, we Indians do name our children after events that occur at the moment of birth. Why do you ask this question, _ _ _ ."*)

Ink Pen

1. We never thought there was any question as to what one filled a pen with. *Ink* seemed the logical thing to put into a pen. But the people of Pittsburgh must be unsure of that since they feel the need to specify that the contents of a pen be ink. Perhaps they have found out that a lot of people fill their pens with substances other than ink.

Maybe *The Pittsburgh Press* TV review person fills his pens with acid? Maybe the residents of **Scroll Hill** fill their pens with chicken soup and the residents of Polish Hill fill their pens with sauerkraut juice? Perhaps the ironworkers fill their pens with **Arn** (the red hot kind or the yellow sudsy kind)? And maybe the captain of the Gateway Clipper Fleet fills his pen with water from the Mon River?

Ink Pen? Well, why not. Sure takes the guesswork out of knowing what's in the pen when someone hands you one.

Use this space for making smart-aleck comments about our work . . . or for composing your own submissions for Volume II.

Jag, Jag Around

1. To tease, joke around, torment (usually) in a friendly manner.

2. To get stabbed by a *jagger*. See: *Jagger*

Jagger

1. A sharp lip that grows in the rock music industry and on which many females have found themselves impaled.

2. A sharp spine that grows on flowers and plants, such as roses and cacti. A whole bush full of *jaggers* is called, sensibly enough, a *jagger bush*.

Jagger is a much more interesting word than the word - *thorn* - for which it substitutes. Consider these possibilities, had the principals involved, been real Pittsburghers.

A certain famous author might have titled his well known novel, *"The **Jagger** Birds."*

Old Will Shakespeare would have said, in Hamlet, *"Leave her to heaven. And to these **jaggers** that in her bosom lodge, To prick and sting her."*

William Jennings Bryan might have said *"You shall not press down upon the brow of labor this crown of **jaggers**."*

And finally, a former Governor, now a former U.S. Attorney General, and would-be senator might have been named Attorney General ***Jaggerburgh***.

Jagoff

1. Unpleasant individual, jerk. As in *"I waited in the ticket line for 20 minutes and just as I got to the window that **jagoff** ticket agent*

put down the 'out to lunch' sign and walked away."

Jaynell

1. The former J & L Steel Mill, now the site of a small building and lots of grass.

Jumbo

1. Dumbo, the elephant's, long lost brother.

2. What every woman wants, but few ever get.

3. Baloney (or bologna, if you prefer) in Pittsburgh. Perhaps originating from the fact that, as compared to salami and other delicatessen meats bologna is frequently very large in diameter.

Jynt Iggle

1. A place where an absolute maximum bird offers you absolute minimum pricing. See also, *Absolute Minimum Pricing*.

Use this space for making smart-aleck comments about our work . . . or for composing your own submissions for Volume II.

Kairk

1. The sound you hear issuing from the throats of thousands of Pittsburghers as they arise in the mornings and clear their lungs of the sinus-clogging Pittsburgh air that has accumulated overnight.

2. The pronunciation of the last name of a well known ship's captain, by the Romulan Ambassador.

3. The way Pittsburghers pronounce the name of their neighborhood, Carrick.

KD

1. The first two call letters of radio station KDKA, owned by Westinghouse Broadcasting and having the distinction of being the first commercial FM radio station in the United

States. See also: **K-Team.**

K-Team

1. A Pittsburgh team, somewhat like another team of television fame, with a similiar sounding name, except only bigger and louder. See also: **Shakespeare.**

Keller

1. A famous person who is the subject of bad jokes about blind people.

2. This is the Pittsburgh pronunciation of the word *color*. It is derived from a combination of the words *kelly* and *color*. The word *kelly* was used in Pittsburgh's early history by the Irish, who were among the area's first settlers, to denote the word *green*. The word **keller** evolved this way: first the Irish simply used the word *kelly* to mean *green*. Then the non-Irish expanded it to *kelly green* (since a lot of them couldn't remember just exactly which color, *kelly* was supposed to be). Teachers of that era,

wanting to be certain there was no confusion, added the word *color* to the phrase, so Pittsburghers would say *kelly green color*. And, of course, with Pittsburghers' penchant for dropping syllables - even whole words - the phrase got shortened to **keller** which eventually came to be a synonym for *color - any* color, not just green.

If you believe any of what you just read, we have a large bridge in Aliquippa we'd like to sell you, real cheap.

Ken

1. What every Barbie doll wants.

2. One of the authors of this book.

3. *Can,* as said by a Pittsburgher, as in the interrogative *"**Ken** you come with me?"* That phrase should be distinguished from the imperative, *"**Ken.** You come with me!"* And from Barbie's question: *"**Ken, ken** you come with me?"*

Kennywood

1. The "Disneyland" of Pittsburgh, complete with talking trash cans and strolling cartoon characters. Open during the summer months and well known to thousands of teens whose college education was made possible, in part, by summer employment there.

Kernegie

1. The town where Andrew Carnegie [1835 - 1919] lived and which was named for him. The town is famous for providing a well known riddle as follows: Is the correct pronunciation of its name "Ker-nay´-gie," which is how its residents pronounce the name, or is "Car´-nah-gie," which is how the rest of the world pronounces it? Well, Andrew isn't around to tell us; but knowledgeable people - from **Kernegie** of course - advise us that Mr. Carnegie insisted on using the pronunciation he grew up with in his hometown of Dunfermline, Scotland - Ker-nay´-gie.

Ketch

1. What the Pirates and the Steelers offense should be doing.

Kitchen Chair

1. An unusual type of parking meter used by Pittsburghers to hold their parking places when their cars are *not* in them.

Klondikes

1. Klingon women who dress in men's clothing.

2. A chunk of vanilla ice cream covered with a crunchy chocolate coating, introduced by the Isaly Company many years ago. Often imitated, but never equalled, this is a staple food item for Pittsburghers, young and old.

Krogering

1. A place Pittsburghers can no longer go.

Lay Out

1. What you do with dear, departed Uncle Harry, so everyone can have a last visit with him at the funeral home.

2. What you do, especially if you're young and female, when the sky is blue, the sun is out and you've got a big beach towel to *lay out* on. This usage arises perhaps from the associated phrase, *cook out*, in that the results of *laying out* too long, resemble the charred meat one can get when the fire is up too high and on too long.

Left

1. There go those Pittsburghers again, adding letters in strange places. You see, when some Pittsburghers say "*I left him in,*" they don't mean that "he" was already inside, and

"I" allowed him to stay there. Instead they mean "he" was outside and "I" allowed him to enter. When and why the *f* was added to *let* turning it into **left** is unknown.

Lie´-berry

1. If it weren't for Andrew Carnegie, Pittsburghers probably wouldn't use this word. During his lifetime Andrew Carnegie donated millions of dollars as endowments for libraries throughout the Country. All over the United States, such a building is called a *library*; in Pittsburgh it is called a **lieberry**. So much for the pronunciation guide at the bottom of each page of the dictionaries in those **lieberries.**

Liberty Avenue

1. A street in Pittsburgh said by some to be not unlike the *red light* districts of Boston, Baltimore and other American cities. The city of Pittsburgh is working hard to get rid of the ladies of the evening who ply their trade in that area by converting the buildings

to cultural centers. Will these shady ladies change their ways and become upstanding members of society? Well, that might just happen. After all, look at Julia Roberts, of *Pretty Woman*. But then again, that's a whorse of a different color.

Light Up Night

1. Pittsburgh's gift to tourists, local photographers and the electric utility companies, during which various *dahntahn* office buildings keep their lights on at night producing a very photogenic display and using enough electricity to power Switzerland for a year. Frequently coincides with Thanksgiving weekend.

Little Worshington

1. There is no *big* Worshington but there *is* a Washington, D.C. and that is what *Little Worshington* is a smaller version of. *Little Worshington*, also known as *Worshington* "Pee-Ā" or as outsiders might

say it, "Washington, Pennsylvania," has many disadvantages compared to its big-city cousin.

For example *Little Worshington* gets none of the National attention that results from the fact that its big-city cousin is so deeply enmeshed in politics and drugs. *Little Worshington* receives none of the money that flows freely from the Federal Government on account of the grinding poverty in which its big-city cousin's residents find themselves. *Little Worshington* receives none of the publicity generated by the activities of its distinguished elected officials, as does its big-city cousin because of its former mayor, Marion Berry.

Poor, poor *Little Worshington*!

Lozengers
See: *Tempachur*

L R T

1. Acronym for *Light Rail Transit*, the mass transit system opened in 1985, which makes part of its runs underground, through ***dahntahn Pixburgh***, and above ground on the ***Souseside***. Now called the "***T***".

Use this space for making smart-aleck comments about our work . . . or for composing your own submissions for Volume II.

Mace

1. A large club, used in medieval times, to beat serfs over the head, as a means of extracting an oath of fealty to their political leaders. Failure to give this oath frequently led to the serf's loss of life.

2. A large club, used in modern times, to hold over the heads of municipal employees, as a means of extracting gifts of money for their political leaders. Failure to give this money frequently leads to the employee's loss of livelihood.

Mahnt Troy

1. When the Greeks weren't able to mount Troy, their leader told them to quit being so serious and start horsing around. The rest is history.

2. Diphthongs and sinuses combine to result in this pronunciation of one of Pittsburgh's neighborhoods.

Mayor

1. A hereditary position similiar in power and authority to that of the Pharaohs in ancient Egypt, which position is held by a designated Democrat in Pittsburgh.

Mayview

1. A Pittsburgh institution

Meer

1. A *meer* is a bright, silvery object, made in all sizes and shapes and used especially by women. Reflect on that, Pittsburghers.

Melk

1. That white stuff that we never outgrew our need for, that goes great with cold cereal, chocolate chip cookies and ulcers.

Mellon Bank

1. Pittsburgh's largest bank, with many branches, excoriated by many, a few years ago, for taking Pittsburgh depositors' money and investing it in foreign countries instead of in local ventures, and which suffered monumental losses when many of those investments went bad, thus bringing to mind an old quote about *just desserts.*

Member

1. In their usual fashion Pittsburghers dropped the beginning of the word *remember* to turn it into **member.** Of course, it could also refer to a person who has joined a group or one of the omnipresent **clubs** which were described earlier in this book. Or it could be a part of the body. Thus, with all these meanings to choose from we could look forward to such gems as: *"Hey Jack,* **member** *the new* **member***; he got* **dis-membered** *when he was hit by a train."*

Merried

1. A Pittsburgh word for the state of marital bliss that many couples find themselves in. It is derived from the word *merry*. Language sure is a funny thing, isn't it.

Michelle

1. Michelle Madoff, member of Pittsburgh City Council, known affectionately, (or otherwise) simply as **Michelle** by many. Frequently the source of, or at least the center of, controversy, on matters before Council, she is lauded by many for efforts at de-politicizing normally political matters. A walking, talking example of the phrase, *"you either love her or you hate her."*

2. Definitely *not* Eugene de Pasquale's belle.

Midfield Terminal

1. An airport in search of a name. (People who fly have an aversion to being in, or near, anything with the word *terminal* in it.

Mill (See also: *Still Mill*)

1. A place where steel was made in Pittsburgh. Meaning now obsolete.

2. A selection of foodstuffs served at a table as described by a Pittsburgher, as in *"You can get a **rilly** good **mill** at that new place over in **the Strip**."* (See also: ***rilly*** and ***mill***.)

The Mon

1. What Pittsburghers call the Monongahela River when they don't have time to slow down their talking to enunciate all the syllables clearly. May be derived from an old Indian word meaning *"Big-water-that-comes-suddenly-in-the-Spring-thaw-and-turns-White-Man's-fancy-boats-into-kindling-ha-ha-ha."*

Morning Drive

1. The period between 6:30 a.m. and 9:00 a.m. during which area motorists are treated to a steady stream of radio personality banter, traffic reports and commercials for car dealers, interspersed with occasional musical interludes.

Nebby

1. A mildly chiding word, **nebby** is one of those quintessential Pittsburgh words and means *nosey*. It is generally used between friends, or between adults and children and so it is usually a more nearly polite word than *nosey*. A person who is **nebby** is (depending on who they are, their relationship to the person calling them **nebby**, and the number of years they have been taking karate lessons) a **neb**, a **nebnose** or a **nebs** _ _ **t**.

Neo Gothic

1. An example of one of many colorful Pittsburgh terms derived from the languages of the ethnic groups that populate the City. This word is used to describe Pittsburgh's architectural

masterpiece, PPG Place. **Neo Gothic** is derived from the Greek **neos**, meaning *new*, and the Latin **Gothic**, meaning *godawful amount of glass.*

New Jersey

1. One of the 50 United States and Pennsylvania's neighbor to the east. The nickname of New Jersey is supposed to be *The Garden State*; however it is obvious that this name resulted from a typographical error, as anyone who has driven through the state with their car windows down, can tell you. The actual nickname is *The Garbage State.*

2. What everyone on the Penguins Hockey Team (and all their fans) will need in the Fall of 1992, when they introduce their new logo.

Norseside

1. Similar to **Souseside**, but on the other side of the rivers.

North Fursales

1. In France it's *Versailles* pronounced "Vair-sigh´." In Pittsburgh, it's *Versailles*, which they sometimes pronounce "Ver-sales´," but which, as it flies off their lips, usually ends up coming out as, **Fur-salés**. Must be a lot of muskrats running around there.

Nuh-uhh´

1. Like its cousin, Yuh-huh´, this word, if you want to call it that, is also quintessential **Pittsburghese**. It means *no*, but it is not a simple exclamation as in, *nope*. Rather **nuh-uhh´**, pronounced with the accent on the **uhh**, is more like, *"No way, José,"* or *"No, no, you can't fool me,"* or *"You've got to be kidding!"* For example, if someone says to you, *"I just heard that Mr. Rogers was trying out for shortstop on the Pirates,"* an appropriate response for anyone but a Pittsburgher might be *"I truly find that suggestion very hard to believe and I sincerely doubt if it is actually true."* A

Pittsburgher, on the other hand, in their own loquacious manner, says it all very succinctly with one word: **Nuh-uhh´**.

Use this space for making smart-aleck comments about our work . . . or for your own submissions for Volume II.

Ohiopyle

1. The name of the geographic area in which is located, *Fallingwater*, the unique house designed by world famous architect, Frank Lloyd Wright, for Edgar Kaufmann. The word ***Ohiopyle*** was adopted by Mr. Kaufmann from one of the Indian languages and means: *"Whoa-Betsy-this-is-**not**-what-I-meant-when-I-said-the-house-should-have-running-water."*

Use this space for making smart-aleck comments about our work . . . or for composing your own submissions for Volume II.

Parkway, The

1. A long stretch of concrete, extending from Monroeville to the Airport, so named because the Pennsylvania Dept. of Transportation has arranged free parking on it from 6:30 a.m. to 9:00 a.m. and 4:30 p.m. to 6:30 p.m. Monday through Friday, year-'round.

2. A highway specifically designed by engineers as a working example of the phrase, *"you can't get there from here."*

3. A 25 mile long construction zone broken up by small sections of usable highway.

4. A maze, such as is found in puzzle books, where the object is to start on one side and by traveling a tortuous, circuitous path with numerous detours and dead ends, find the

only open exit on the other side.

Parkway East, Parkway West, Inbound & Outbound

1. In their (largly successful) efforts to confuse visitors to their City, Pittsburghers use these terms to refer to portions of the Parkway and direction of travel. The naming is designed in the manner of *"All roads lead to Rome"* where *Pittsburgh* replaces *Rome*. The ***Parkway East*** is the section from Pittsburgh, eastward to Monroeville. So, if you are driving from Pittsburgh toward Monroeville, you are on the ***Parkway East, outbound***. If you are in Monroeville driving toward Pittsburgh, you are on the ***Parkway East, inbound***. Clever readers as you no doubt are, you have already figured that the ***Parkway West*** is the section from Pittsburgh to the Airport. So if you are in Pittsburgh, driving toward the airport, you are on the ***Parkway West, outbound***; and if you are in the airport area, driving toward Pittsburgh,

you are on the **_Parkway West, inbound_**.
See, wasn't that simple.

PAT

1. The second part, of the first name, of a
bunch of Pittsburgh girls with the unique
name, *Mary Pat.* This combination is rarely
found anywhere else in the world.

2. Acronym for **P**ort **A**uthority **T**ransit.

3. A joke played by the people of Pittsburgh
upon themselves, in which an organization
with little authority attempts to arrange
scheduled transit over non-water routes.

Pataydas

1. A member of the tuber family, this food
product is usually brown in color and
ellipsoid in shape. In Pittsburgh households,
frequently served with steak and **_Arn_**.

Patition

1. One of several incorrect ways of spelling
petition.

2. As pronounced in Pittsburgh, a wall which divides one room from another.

Peeps

1. What a Peeping Tom tries for lots of.

2. A word heard most often around Easter time, referring to baby chicks.

Pellow

1. One of those white, fluffy things that you stick under youe head when you go to sleep.

Penguin

1. A cute but tough little creature, dressed in black and white, functioning best on the ice, and occupying a position of prominence in the Pittsburgh Zoo.

2. A cute but tough little creature, dressed in black and gold, functioning best on the ice and occupying a position of prominence in Pittsburgh's Civic Arena.

Penn-Lincoln Parkway

1. The real name of *The Parkway,* parts of which are identified by various numerical designations for purposes of "ease" of description. Such designations include: *376, 279,* and *22-30.* Other alpha-numeric designations that have been suggested for the Parkway include:

$$\sqrt{0}, \quad \sum_{-\infty}^{+\infty} \Delta t, \quad \text{and } 666$$

Pennsylvania Dutch

1. Most Pittsburghers have visited the area around Lancaster, Pennsylvania and that's the area that most of the State's *Pennsylvania Dutch* call home. As you would expect, of course, *Pennsylvania Dutch* is a misnomer - none of them is Dutch and their forefathers came, not from Holland, in the 17th and 18th centuries, but rather from Germany. Thus, it is the Pennsylvania *Deutsch* that inhabited central Pennsylvania and that word - *Deutsch* - was changed to the

more pronounceable, and easy to remember, although, totally incorrect - **Dutch**.

Pennsylvania Dutch speech is colorful and amusing since it is usually half English and half German, all assembled according to the German rules of syntax - which require word order in a sentence to be entirely different from what it is in English.

It is the **Pennsylvania Dutch** we owe for one of the most common **Pittsburghese** words - **redd up** - which means to tidy up or clean up, as in, *"Company's coming, I'd better* **redd up** *the kitchen."*

PG

1. Acronym commonly, used for *The Post Gazzette*, Pittsburgh's morning newspaper, published Monday through Saturday. *The Post Gazette* maintains an unusual arrangement with Pittsburgh's other major newspaper. *The Pittsburgh Press*, whereby

both papers share the same classified advertising staff and printing facilities and plant, but have totally separate editorial and space advertising staffs and ownership.

Philadelphia

1. Remember the old saying about a person so ugly that *"he had a face that only a mother could love?"* Well, that's how Pittsburghers feel about **Philadelphia**... or, *Filthydelphia* as Pittsburghers "affectionately" call it.

   The fact is, Pittsburghers, gentle folks that they are, are embarassed by the fact that **Philadelphia** is in *their* state. Their most fervent wish is that **Philadelphia** would be moved to another state. Georgia, for example. *Soviet* Georgia!

Pigeon

1. A member of our avian society that inhabits

the window ledges of Pittsburgh office buildings in areas of the City where Pittsburghers are willing to throw them scraps of bread and **pupcorn**. Fondly referred to, by Bill Burns, the well known KDKA news anchor, as *"rats with wings."*

Pitcher

1. A *pitcher* (ceramic, with handles), or a *pitcher* (flesh and blood, with bat), or in Pittsburgh, a *pitcher* (photograph, black and white, or color.)

William Pitt

1. Statesman and explorer, **William Pitt** sought peace and quiet by settling in Western Pennsylvania, whereupon he was set upon by the Indians, the French, the British, and others not favorably disposed toward a settlement in the area. Getting disgusted with these disruptions, to say nothing of the arrows and bullets whizzing by his head, old Bill Pitt expressed his displeasure by making, the now famous, statement, *"This burgh is the pits"*; whence arises the name of our town.

Pittsburg

1. There's one in Kansas and there's another one in California but you won't find one of these in Western Pennsylvania.

Pittsburgh, City of Champions

1. A sometime contradiction in terms.

2. Formerly, Edward DeBartolo's fondest dream.

Pixburgh

1. The way some Pittsburghers pronounce the name of their native land. It is many of these same *Pixburghers* who *aks* questions instead of asking them.

Poosh

1. A dog *(pooch),* as pronounced by a Frenchman with a lisp.

2. The opposite of pull.

Pop

1. Something that weasels do when in the vicinity of a mulberry bush.

2. A term of endearment for someones father or grandfather; in particular, for those of you who remember it, what Charlie Chan was called by his Number 1 son.

3. A Pittsburgher's word for what folks from the East call *soda* - a carbonated, usually flavored, beverage. This is a very confusing term when used, as it frequently is, in conjunction with other words. For example:

> ***Pop*** Can. Your fathers behind or, behind your fathers bathroom.

> ***Pop*** Machine - A device for mechanically producing fathers or for mechanically producing carbonated beverages for fathers to drink.

> Diet ***Pop*** - A skinny father.

Pound
1. A unit of measure. In England it is used to measure weight and monetary value. In the

United States it is used to measure the sale of *Deal-A-Meal* cards, *Sweatin' to the Oldies* tapes, and cans of *Slim-Fast*.

2. In Pittsburgh, a place for homeless dogs, which can be adopted by new owners for a small fee.

3. In Pittsburgh, a place for homeless cars which can be re-adopted by current owners for an astronomical fee.

Presby

1. Nickname for Presbyterian University Hospital, located in the Oakland section of Pittsburgh. Known for its pioneering organ transplant research and its top quality hospital cafeteria whose specialty of the house is *Liver Surprise*.

The Press

1. The commonly used name of one of Pittsburgh's two major newspapers, correctly known as ***The Pittsburgh Press***.

The Press is published 6 days a week and Sundays. It is known as Pittsburgh's "evening" newspaper; however the first edition is usually on the newstands before noon. The Sunday edition has a circulation of some 550,000 and is characterized by a large number of advertising inserts, bound together by larger (or smaller) sections of news and sports. See also: **PG**

Punkin

1. Something small and cute, as in *"Come to Daddy, **punkin**."*

2. Something large and orange, as in *"Oh, what a big **punkin** you got for Halloween, dear."*

3. A bad joke one of your relatives tells...like this one.

Punxsutawney

1. A small town in Western Pennsylvania which was given its name by the Algonquin and

Lenape tribes. The name translates loosely *(very, very loosely)* as: *"Place-in-the-woods-where-little-men-with-big-cameras-try-to-converse-with-furry-brown-four-legged-creature."*

The little creature in question is a groundhog and his name is Phil. Local legend has it that if Phil comes out of his burrow on February 2nd and sees his shadow, he will emit a groundhoglike sound and return to his burrow, signifying that six more weeks of winter are to be expected. Pittsburghers, being wiser than their country brethern, don't believe a word of this nonsense and have indicated such by describing Phil in the words of William Shakespeare: *"Full of sound, and furry, signifying nothing."*

Pupcorn

1. A canine affliction of the pedal extremites.

2. A gold colored food product which, when purchased at area motion picture theaters,

costs about the same per ounce as the substance of which it is the same color.

Putzie, Putzie Around

1. A phrase which means *putter around*, usually but not always, with something mechanical, as in, *"My car developed this pinging sound so I think I'll go **putzie around** under the hood to see what's causing it."* Or, *"I just got a new saber saw for my birthday so I'm going downstairs and **putzie around** in the toolroom."*

Don't confuse this phrase with *sputzie around* which means that a sparrow has been sighted. See also: ***Sputzie***

Caution: Do not use this phrase around persons fluent in Yiddish unless you enunciate *very* distinctly.

Quinn and Banana

1. A couple of morning drive radio personalities who apparently weren't listening when their mothers told them: *"If you can't say something nice about a person, don't say anything at all."*

Use this space for making smart-aleck comments about our work . . . or for composing your own submissions for Volume II.

Redd Up
See: ***Pennsylvania Dutch***

Redlight
1. When Pittsburghers give directions they don't use phrases such as *"Turn left at the intersection,"* or even *"Turn left at the traffic light."* In fact, as far as Pittsburghers are concerned, Pittsburgh has no intersections and no traffic lights - or at least no traffic lights of the green or yellow persuasion. Pittsburgh has only *red* traffic lights. So all directions are given in terms of **redlights**, as in *"Go two blocks to the* **redlight***, hang a left, go one more block and then turn left again at the* **redlight** *and you're there."*

Please also note the special spelling -

redlight, which is one word, rather than *red light*, which is two words. If it were spelled with two words, the word *Red* would be an adjective modifying *Light* and one might draw the erroneous conclusion that there were other types of lights - such as, say, green or yellow. That, of course, would be entirely incorrect; there is only one kind of light and that is a *redlight* - accent on the *red*. With all those *redlights* it's a wonder Pittsburghers get past the first block, much less to their final destination.

Renaissance I

1. A world famous magic trick wherein a magician named David Lawrence passed some old buildings through a fire and turned them into a modern office complex.

Renaissance II

1. A magic trick similiar to Renaissance I, except money was used in place of fire.

Right Turn On Red

1. Refers to a law valid throughout Pennsylvania (including Pittsburgh) which permits vehicular traffic to make a right turn after coming to a full stop at a **redlight**. The law was originally passed at the behest of traffic sign manufacturers who have made a fortune selling signs that say "No right turn on red."

Rillize

1. It's too hard for Pittsburghers to say *ree´-a-lize*, so they say **rillize** instead.

Rilly

1. **Rilly** rhymes with silly and means *really*. Imagine the result of telling someone named William that you had a craving for one of those special confections from Dairy Queen. *("I rilly want a Dilly, Billy.")* Or telling your girlfriend that she did something dumb. *("That was rilly silly, Milly.")* Or commenting to a famous skier about the treacherous terrain. *(" That was rilly, hilly, Killy.")* or . . . well, you get the idea.

River Road

1. A vehicular artery in which one frequently finds Pittsburghers caught in the early morning rush to beat the early morning rush hour traffic *or* caught in the late morning rush to beat the late morning rush hour traffic.

Robison

1. Remember that we told you that Pittsburghers had an aversion to pronouncing words with two or more consonants side by side? Well here's a great example. Pittsburghers drop the *n* out of *Robinson* and it becomes ***Robison***. As in Jackie ***Robison*** and ***Robison*** Township.

Rozzlin

1. Farms? Heights? It doesn't matter which *Rosslyn* it is, to Pittsburghers they're all ***Rozzlin***.

Use this space for making smart-aleck comments about our work . . . or for composing your own submissions for Volume II.

Sacrificial Lamb

1. A phrase that comes to mind when describing Pittsburgh's Republican candidate in each mayoral election.

Sammich

1. An edible product invented by a nobleman of the same name *(The Earl of Sammich)* in anticipation of the invention of another gastronomic delight, *chippedchopped ham.*

Scroll Hill

1. One of Pittsburgh's neighborhoods, said to be so named because many of its residents can be found, on a Saturday morning, in their places of worship, reading in a foreign tongue, from scrolls.

Sec´-a-terry

1. One of Pittsburghers' more well known dislikes is the letter *R*, especially when it appears after a consonant, or, God forbid, after another *R*. Such atrocities as **lieberry** (for *library*) and **secaterry** (for *secretary*) are the result. One individual with whom we are acquainted can become the life of the party simply by attempting to say the word *rural*, three times, quickly.

All kidding aside (yeah, sure) **secaterry** is the well known version of *secretary*, as pronounced by many Pittsburgh businessmen. Unless of course, the **secaterry** goes home with the businessman at night, in which case she is his **sexaterry**. Getting paid extra for her special talents gives rise (no pun intended, of course) to the well known phrase, *"It's a business doing pleasure with you."*

Shardin

1. Can you say *Sher´-a-den?* Many

Pittsburghers specially those living there, don't like to. So they say it fast and nasally, and it comes out **Shardin**.

Shahrs

1. Stumped? Just remember this oft quoted phrase: *"April **shahrs** bring May **flahrs**."* And speaking of **shahrs**, don't forget that Pittsburghers don't *take* **shahrs** they **get** them.

Shakespeare

1. The K-Team's favorite playwrite (because of the famous words from Hamlet's soliloquoy . . . *"full of sound and fury, Cigna-fying something."*)

'Sliberty

1. Those syllable sliding, diphthong dropping, Pittsburghers have done it again. Here we have a place that anyone west of the Allegheny River calls *East Liberty*. But in Pittsburgh it's spit out at the speed of an F-16 in a steep dive - **'Sliberty!**

Slippy

1. Many Pittsburghers have an aversion to using any more syllables than they absolutely have to . . . and in fact, use a lot fewer than they should. Many perfectly sensible Pittsburghers say **slippy** instead of *slippery.* Fortunately, it has not gone so far as to produce such roadside warning signs as: **Slippy When Wet;** or popular tunes such as: **Slippy Sliding Away.**

Smiffilled Street Bridge

1. What do Smurfs and Pittsburghers have in common? Well in the middle of January, when it gets really cold, both are blue. But all year 'round both Smurfs and Pittsburghers love the letter *F.*

   The Smurfs like the letter *F* because it is the last letter of their name.

   Pittsburghers like the letter *F* because it is so much easier to pronounce than *TH,* especially when the *TH* comes after an *F.*

Hence our famous bridge and street are often pronounced **Smiffilled** instead of Smithfield. Of course, if it were a warm summer day and the Smurfs were out in force, rushing from Station Square into **dahntahn** Pittsburgh it would be the **Smurffilled** Bridge. . . .

Snik Snaks
1. Little things you eat when you are hungry and it isn't mealtime yet. Does this make a chocolate bar snack a *Snickers snack?*

Soffell, Mrs.
1. A pioneering penologist whose innovative experimentation in prison work release was glamorized by a California motion picture firm.

Souseside
1. The area of Pittsburgh to the South of the Monongahela river. From the Latin **Souse** meaning *many taverns,* and the Greek **side** meaning *over there.*

Spicket

1. The metal thing with the hole on the end that water comes out of.

Spirit

1. Who?

Sputzies

1. An unusual construction, even for Pittsburghers. A hint as to its meaning may be had by noting the following "quotations."

*"A **sputzie** in the hand is worth two in the bush"* (Apologies to Cervantes)

*"Who sees with equal eye, a God of all, A hero perish or a **sputzie** fall."* (Apologies to Alexander Pope)

"Who killed Cock Robin?"
*"I," said the **sputzie**, "with my bow and arrow."* (Apologies to Anonoymous, whoever he may be)

*"I watch and am as a **sputzie** alone upon the housetops."* (Apologies to God)

The Stadium
See: ***Three Rivers Stadium***

Steeltown
1. A nickname for Pittsburgh used primarily by a few individuals of advanced age, who are obviously living in the past.

Street Maintenance Dept
1. An obvious misnomer as anyone who has traveled the streets of the City can attest to. However, Pittburghers can consider themselves lucky, when the condition of Pittsburgh's streets is compared with the condition of streets of other major cities, such as Washington, D.C. *(where the streets are littered with bodies)*, San Francisco *(where the streets are littered with pieces of buildings and broken up baseball stadiums, left over from the last earthquake)*, Detroit *(where the streets are littered with parts of*

recently departed Cosa Nostra members whose financial philosophies may have differed from those of the majority), and Pennsylvania's very own **Filthydelphia** *(where the streets are littered with litter).*

Stillers

1. Pittsburgher's resident football team. In past years their cry was *"one for the thumb,"* (*i.e.,* win another Super Bowl and thereby receive a Super Bowl ring for the remaining un-ringed finger, the thumb). Lately, according to some local sportscasters, the cry should be more like *"don't be all thumbs . . . ."*

Still Mill

1. Excuse me, what was that? See also: **Mill**

Streecar

1. That little steel wheeled, track riding, people moving device that people in other parts of the Country call a *trolley.* Banished from Pittsburgh some years ago, **streecars** are

now mostly just memories of a bygone era. Interestingly enough, although everyone in Pittsburgh called these things **streecars**, examples are found at the Arden **Trolley** Museum. Obviously *those* people have never lived in Pittsburgh.

The Strip (The Strip District)

1. A place **dahntahn** where you'll find just about anything you might want, from souvenirs and novelties to the finest quality meat, fish and fruit, to freshly made fudge and baked goods. But the poor quality counterfeit/fake goods that quit working a week after you buy them - like $50 Rolex watches - can really tick you off.

Subsidence

1. A technical term used by engineers, geologists and coal companies to describe what happens when a great big hole unexpectedly opens up in the ground and swallows your house, your car and your mother-in-law.

Swissvill

1. Would you believe us if we told you that this was a gourmet dish served only in Pittsburgh's finest restaurants, consisting of veal imported from Switzerland?

No? OK, how about a unique Pittsburgh **sammich**, consisting of alternating slices of veal and Swiss cheese topped off with French dressing and a pickle?

Nuh-uhh you say? OK then how about a Pittsburgher's pronunciation of *Swissvale*, a small borough adjacent to Pittsburgh. See also: **Vill.**

Use this space for making smart-aleck comments about our work . . . or for composing your own submissions for Volume II.

T

T

1. A large, short tempered, gold adorned mammal, indigenous to evening television, usually preceded by the modifier, *Mr.*

2. Nickname for the Pittsburgh rail transit system, formerly known as the *L R T* (for *L*ight *R*ail *T*ransit). The name *T* was chosen by the Port Authority Transit as a result of a naming contest; however the nickname is generally regarded as so *un*popular that no one has yet admitted being the winner of the contest. *T* stands for nothing in particular which seems appropriate considering the great lack of enthusiam on the part of the public for that name.

Tamaydas

1. Those round, red things that all parents

know are vegetables . . . until their smart aleck kids come home from college and announce, with an air of superiority, that, botanically speaking, they are really fruit.

Tariffs

1. The rules and regulations by which utilities operate and which define their rates. The tariffs are cleverly constructed by the utilities so that it appears that the cost of the service per kilowatt, per phone call or per cubic foot appears to be quite low; but by the time the consumer adds the billing charge, the line charge, the service charge, the energy cost, and the cost of maintaining the utility company's Executive Beach Club in Jamaica, the total amount on the bill approaches the National Debt.

Telepole

1. A short question and answer session in which your opinon is asked on various subjects, conducted over the telephone.

2. An inexpensive form of communication between individuals in Poland.

3. In Pittsburgh, that big brown log that Bell of Pennsylvania shoves into the pavement and then mounts its communications wires on.

4. A heaven sent gift to the cable television companies of the area.

Tempachur

1. When a Pittsburgher gets sick he may have a fever - or **tempachur**. And if this poor, sick Pittsburgher has a cough he may stop in at the drug store to pick up some **lozengers**.

Tenth Street Bypass

1. An emergency parking lot for barges and other river craft.

Those Ones

1. What you reply when someone says to you:

*"Look at the wallpaper with the number **one** stamped out in all different typestyles. Which **ones** do you like the best?"*

A peculiar (and sometimes annoying) grammatical construction in which Pittsburghers *add* something to a sentence instead of taking it away. Accustomed to the presence of a noun after the word *those* (as in: *those* cars, *those* guys, *those* buildings . . .) they feel obliged to put *something* after the word *those*, even when nothing is needed. So, when a Pittsburgher in a supermarket is asked *"Which apples do you want,"* they reply, pointing to the Red Delicious, *"those ones,"* instead of simply saying *"those."* Needless to say, *those ones* is not restricted to use in the supermarket.

Three Rivers Arts Festival

1. A Pittsburgh event, very similiar to the Indian Rain Dance, in that both of these things bring on rain in unending torrents over a ten day period.

2. A place where artists and artisans, and critics and consumers, all get together to see who's who and what's new, in art in Pittsburgh.

3. A place where the purchase of a $9 t-shirt in considered an acceptable substitute for the purchase of a $900 painting.

Three Rivers Stadium

1. A large public arena erected to serve several functions:

   a. Obtaining revenue from persons attending sporting events conducted therein.

   b. Collecting fees from use of its parking lots.

   c. Selling beer and hot dogs at prices which could lead one to believe they were buying fine wine and filet mignon.

   Not necessarily in that order.

Tile

1. A hard ceramic material found in many bathrooms all over the world.

2. A soft, fluffy, highly absorbent material used for drying faces and hands, found in many Pittsburgh bathrooms.

To Be

1. The first two words of a famous soliloquoy, uttered by an equally famous character, in an equally famous play, written by a, more than equally famous English playwrite.

2. Two words which are as extinct as the Dodo Bird in the vocabulary of most Pittsburghers who say such things as *"The car needs fixed,"* instead of *"The car needs **to be** fixed."* Pittsburghers can drive a high school English teacher to distraction when they combine the lack of the infinitive with Pittsburghese expressions, as in *"The **lieberry** book needs returned."* (No doubt it was a book about English grammar.) It

is not certain where all the missing *to be's* are, but one observer swears that he saw a whole tractor trailer full of them being unloaded at the offices of a Philadelphia lawyer.

Traffic Light

1. An electrical device used at Pittsburgh intersections for traffic control. This device signals drivers of vehicles through use of a series of lights and arrows having the following meanings.

Green Light: Damn the torpedoes, full speed ahead. God help any pedestrians still in the crosswalk.

Yellow Light: Be prepared to stop if a pedestrian or car passes in front of you. Only 26 more vehicles may pass through the intersection before all traffic must stop.

Red Light: Same as yellow light except only 12 more vehicles may pass through the intersection before all traffic must stop.

Green Arrow: A comic book character which appears in the traffic signal to indicate that you may turn left or right across oncoming traffic while praying that said oncoming traffic has a red light at the same time you have your green arrow.

Tubes

1. Pittsburgh slang for tunnels. There are three main tunnels through which vehicular traffic can pass on its way to, or through, Pittsburgh. These tunnels are the *Fort Pitt*, the *Squirrel Hill*, and the *Liberty* Tunnels. Interestingly enough, *only* the Liberty Tunnels are called ***tubes***.

These tunnels are a rich source of stories for journalists who enjoy writing about such events as the tractor trailer drivers who ignore the *overheight* signal at the last exit before the tunnels, and then try - and fail - to squeeze a 12-1/2 foot high trailer through a 12 foot high opening.

Tugboat

1. Small, high powered waterborne craft designed to push large, no powered waterborne craft, such as barges, and to extract said large waterborne craft from inconvenient resting places, such as the bottom of the Monongahela River or the top of the *Tenth Street Bypass*.

Use this space for making smart-aleck comments about our work . . . or for composing your own submissions for Volume II.

Umm´-brella

1. Many Pittsburghers have an aversion to words with emphasis at their middle or end. So, independent souls that they are, Pittsburghers simply alter the pronunciation to suit themselves. Thus, *umbrella* becomes ***umm´-brella***. And *eclipse* becomes ***eee´-clipse***.

USS

1. The chemical symbol for the mixture of iron and other substances to form the material known as *steel.* Now archaic.

Use this space for making smart-aleck comments about our work . . . or for composing your own submissions for Volume II.

Vill

1. As every housewife knows, lamb stew comes from lamb, chicken soup comes from chicken, and *vill* parmesan come from *vill*, presumably a small, four legged creature that spends its time in the pasture, rolling around in patches of cheese and tomato sauce.

Waiting Dinner

1. A phrase usually used by the lady of the house, when you've arrived an hour later than you promised, to describe the delay in serving dinner, because she was waiting for you. For example, *"I was waiting dinner*

until you got home from the office and you were so late we are all starved."

Wait On

1. Similiar to the phrase **waiting dinner**, **wait on** means *wait for* as in "What took you so long to get back? *I've been waiting on you for a half hour."*

We Do It All To You

1. The motto of Pittsburgh's crack team that roams the City looking for parking scoflaws and installs the dreaded Denver McBoot.

Wharf

1. Also, known as the **Mon Wharf** and **Mon Parking Wharf**. A small body of concrete, covered, alternately, by a large body of cars and a larger body of water.

Whole 'Nother

1. Suppose you ate, what you thought, was the very last piece of an apple pie ... and then you found a second, untouched, apple pie in

the refrigerator. You would describe this situation by saying "I found *another whole* apple pie in the refrigerator."

But Pittsburghers don't like that particular grammatical construction - *another whole*. So, as we have pointed out before, Pittsburghers do what comes naturally, - they drop out at least one of the "extra" syllables. And, in this case, to make the remaining syllables flow even more smoothly, they reverse the order of the words, ending up with ***whole 'nother*** instead of *another whole*.

So, our statement now becomes typical Pittsburghese - *"I found a **whole 'nother** pie in the refrigerator."*

Window Seal

1. In the U.S., an elastomeric material laid down around the edges of windows to prevent leaks.

2. In Antarctica, a cute black creature with flippers, which will occasionally crawl onto a window ledge to sit.

3. In Pittsburgh, a portion of a window, known in other parts of the Country as a *window sill.*

Winky's

1. A small, locally based fast food chain whose major claim to fame was that it did not have a restaurant in Wilmerding. Its food was apparently not quite fast enough (or was perhaps *too* fast) since the chain went out of business a few years ago.

Worsh

1. As a noun, it's the stuff that goes into the washing machine when it's dirty.

2. As a verb (***to worsh***) it's what you do with all that stuff once it gets into the washing machine.

The Yock

1. Term used by Pittsburghers to refer to the Youghiogheny River, so called because of the sounds of laughter *("yock, yock, yock")* heard emanating from high school geography teachers reading their students attempts to spell the word correctly. The ~~Yuckioghenie~~ ~~Yugoghany, Yugo-ganny~~ River is a favorite for white water rafting, whence comes its name, which according to Algonquin lore, means: *"Place-in-water-where-White-Man-in-rubber-raft-learn-true-meaning-of-expression 'between-a-rock-and-a-hard-place.'"*

Y'all

1. A southern *yunz*.

You've Got A Friend in Pennsylvania

1. A slogan coined by the Republican administration of Pennsylvania to try to show the Democratic majority of Pittsburgh which side their bread was buttered on.

2. A mythical person for whom many have have searched but none has found.

Yunz

1. Quintessential **Pittsburghese**, and the bane of Pittsburgh educators, this is the word that sets Pittsburghers apart from everyone else in the world. It is also - and how appropriate - an apparent contradiction in terms.

   As explained under **those ones**, Pittsburghers add the word **ones** even when no word is needed. Thus **yunz** is said to be a contraction of *you* and *ones*, a sort of Northern *y'all*. But, **yunz** is singular, with **yunzes** usually reserved for the plural. So, you figure it out.

While **yunz** can be heard every day in many areas of Pittsburgh, it is not considered appropriate for business. The use of **yunz** in combination with other Pittsburghese expressions and inflections can lead to funny - and potentially disastrous - consequences.

Envision a Pittsbugh salesman calling on a major account, in say, Ohio, and extolling the virtues of his company's products by saying: *"I've made a careful examination of your computer system. The paper feed is **crookit**, the hard drive **needs fixed** and your software **needs updated.** I can supply you with a **beeyouteeful** new disc drive - much better than **those ones.** Here's a **pitcher** of it. **Ahiya** is only a short distance from Pittsburgh so service will be no problem at all. I know **yunz** will be happy with us."*

Use this space for making smart-aleck comments about our work . . . or for your own submissions for Volume II.

Z

Zoo

1. A collection of flora and fauna housed in Highland Park and named officially, *The Highland Park Zoo.*

   The Zoo has recently undergone substantial renovation at great expense to ensure that animals formerly easily seen in cages can now easily conceal themselves, behind rocks and vegetation.

2. Another phrase used to describe the meetings of Pittsburgh City Council. See also: ***Circus***.

Zup

1. *Zup. Zup?* **Zup**? Got you stumped? Are you asking, "*what's zup?*" Well, shades of Abbot and Costello. **Zup** is a contraction of most any word ending in the letter *s* plus the

word *up.*

As you already know from these pages Pittsburghers produce more contractions than a roomful of pregnant women. Their philosophy is *why say it clearly and distinctly, using two or three words when you can contract them all together into one tiny little word thrown over the gums and spit out across lips at just under the speed of light?*

Pittsburghers aren't interested in *what's up?* They want to know **zup**?

And, of course, by extension: *"***Zup** *must come down." "***Zup** *to you." "Surf ***zup.***"*

Use this space for making smart-aleck comments about our work . . . or for your own submissions for Volume II.

126

FINAL EXAMINATION

You read the book. Now it's time to see what you've learned. Here, courtesy of James V. Battisti, the man with numerous, humorous contributions, is a test that all readers must take *and pass*, before they are allowed to put this book down. Thanks to Pittsburghers everywhere, for providing us with the great material from which we were able to write this book. See 'ya soon . . . in Volume II.

1. **What is the fastest way to get from *dahntahn* to Monroeville?**
   A) Via Cleveland
   B) Greyhound Bus
   C) The "T"
   D) The Parkway South
   E) You can't get there from here

2. **Where can you find the country's first mail order haircut business?**
   A) Liberty Avenue
   B) Yugoslavia
   C) Souseside
   D) Three Rivers Stadium

3. **Now for a cooking question. Which of the following is *not* a Pittsburgh food?**
   A) Hutzulochka
   B) Babushka
   C) Kielbasi
   D) Sputzie and sauerkraut
   E) Putzie and pork rind

4. **What is the official sport of Pittsburgh?**
   A) Pothole fishing
   B) Pothole dodging
   C) Subway spelunking
   D) Hubcap collecting
   E) All of the above

5. **Who first called Pittsburgh the "melting pot" of the world?**
   A) H.J. Heinz
   B) Chuck Noll
   C) Betty Crocker
   D) William Pitt
   E) Timothy Leary

6. **How can you become a citizen of Pittsburgh?**
   A) Break the world's "Pierogi Eating" record
   B) Sign a patition to boycott infinitives.
   C) Fail this test
   D) Any of the above

7. **Where is Pittsburgh's only nudist colony?**
   A) The subway station in Shadyside
   B) The Strip District
   C) Herr's Island
   D) Where's *what*?

8. **How many Polish people can you fit on a hill?**
   A) Two: one to find it and one to hold the ladder
   B) Three: one to find it, one to hold the ladder and one to keep count
   C) None, it's under construction
   D) Depends on the size of the kielbasi crop

9. **What do you get when you cross a *kava* with a *packi*?**
   A) A rash
   B) Coffee and doughnuts
   C) A three humped camel
   D) A Master's degree in linguistics
   E) A headache

10. **Which attraction in Pittsburgh draws the most visitors?**
    A) The one mile, above ground subway
    B) The City Council Three Ring Circus
    C) The annual "1001 Kazoos" Symphony
    D) The chippedchopped Ham Festival